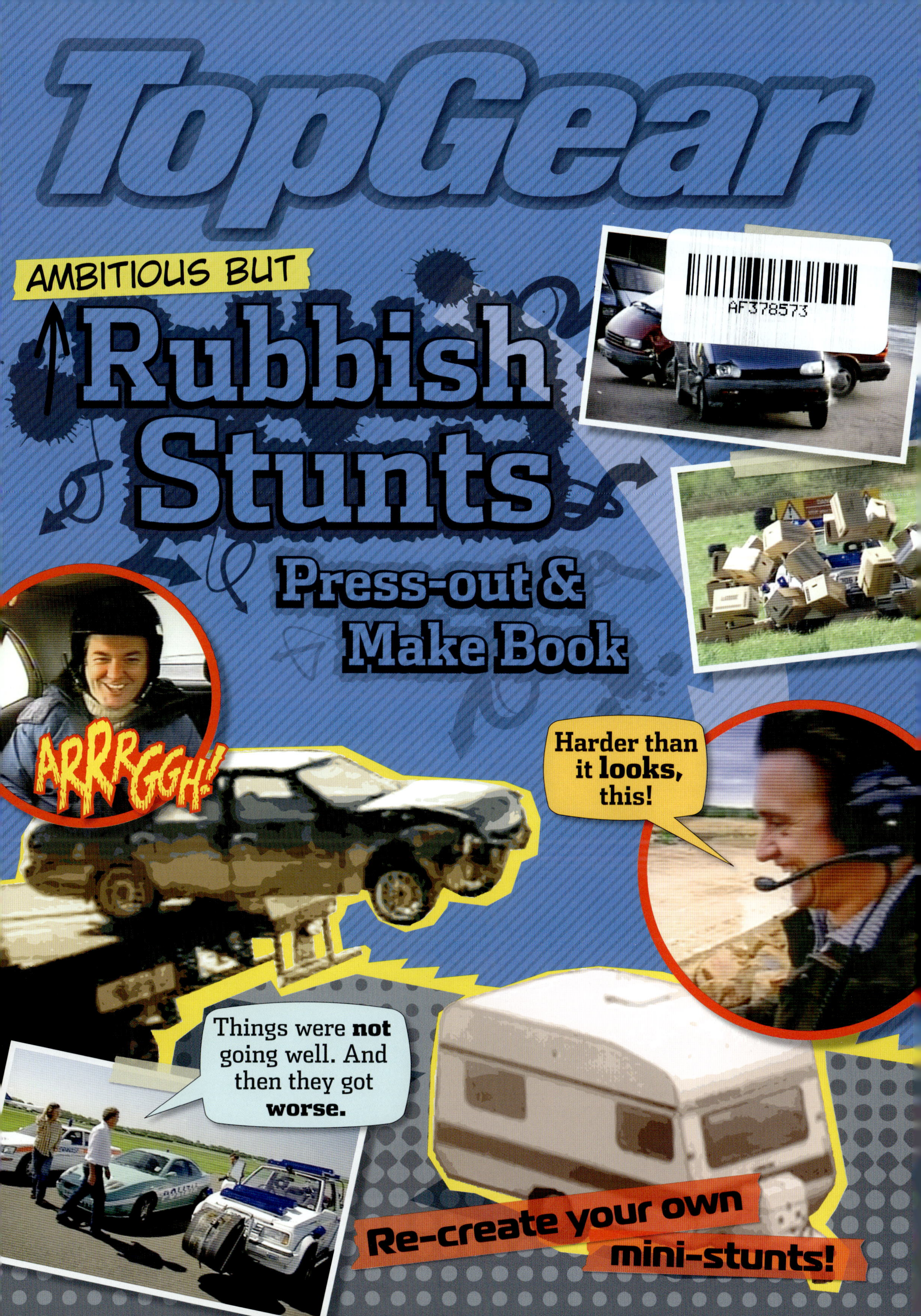
TopGear
AMBITIOUS BUT
Rubbish
Stunts
Press-out &
Make Book
AF378573
ARRRGGH!
Harder than it looks, this!
Things were not going well. And then they got worse.
Re-create your own mini-stunts!

Mad Quotes

Over the years the Top Gear team have got themselves involved in some weird, wonderful but mostly rubbish stunts. And quite often the presenters are so stunned by what's happening that they say some pretty mad things!

Can you match each quote to the correct presenter?

4) Said by:

5) Said by:

1) Said by:

2) Said by:

6) Said by:

3) Said by:

7) Said by:

Spot the Difference

Top Gear invited a nun called Sister Wendy to drive a monster truck… over five cars. And her effort wasn't too rubbish. Can you spot the 8 differences in these two shots of the stunt?

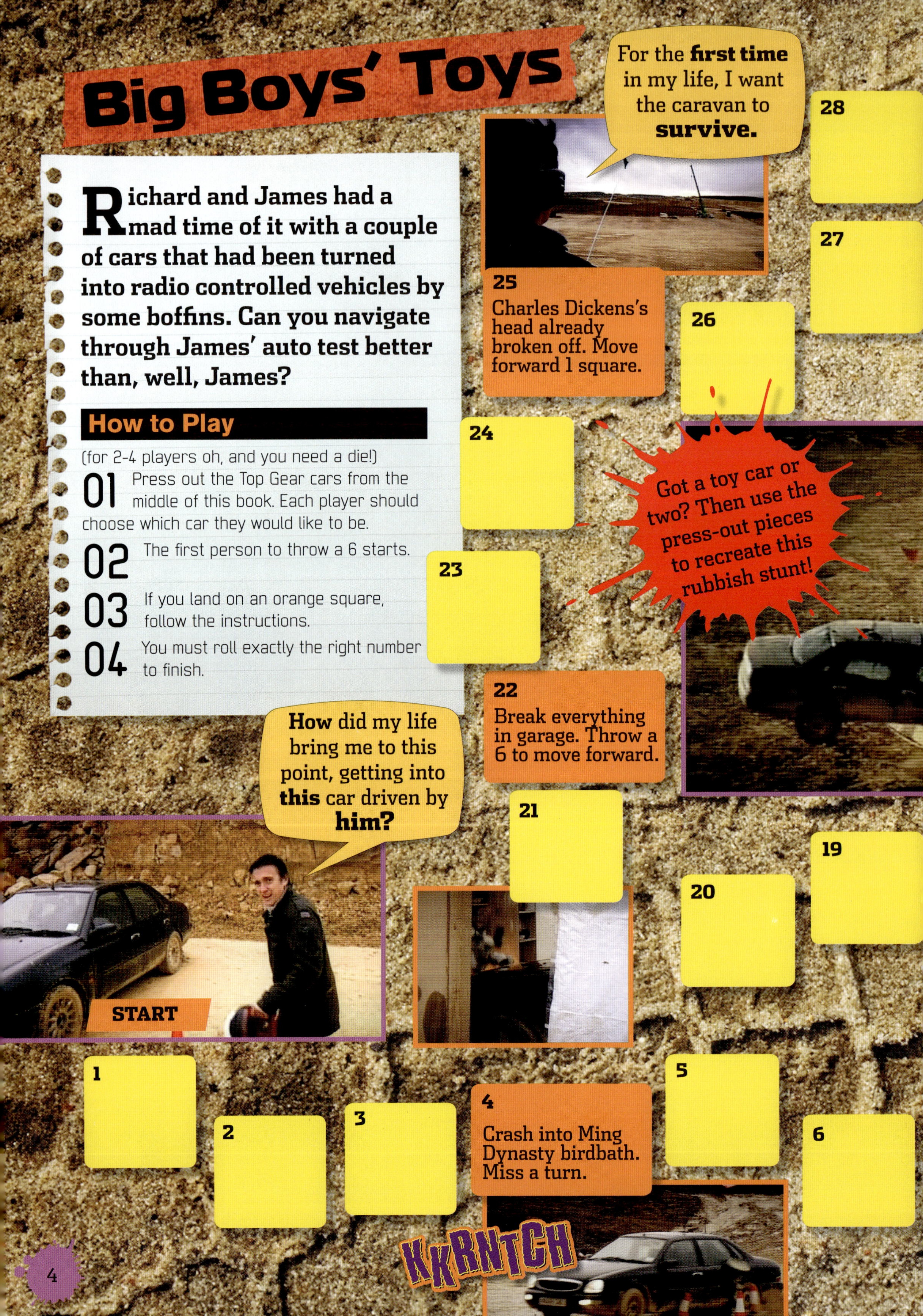

Big Boys' Toys

Richard and James had a mad time of it with a couple of cars that had been turned into radio controlled vehicles by some boffins. Can you navigate through James' auto test better than, well, James?

How to Play

(for 2-4 players oh, and you need a die!)

01 Press out the Top Gear cars from the middle of this book. Each player should choose which car they would like to be.

02 The first person to throw a 6 starts.

03 If you land on an orange square, follow the instructions.

04 You must roll exactly the right number to finish.

28

27

25 Charles Dickens's head already broken off. Move forward 1 square.

26

24

23

22 Break everything in garage. Throw a 6 to move forward.

21

20

19

1

2

3

4 Crash into Ming Dynasty birdbath. Miss a turn.

5

6

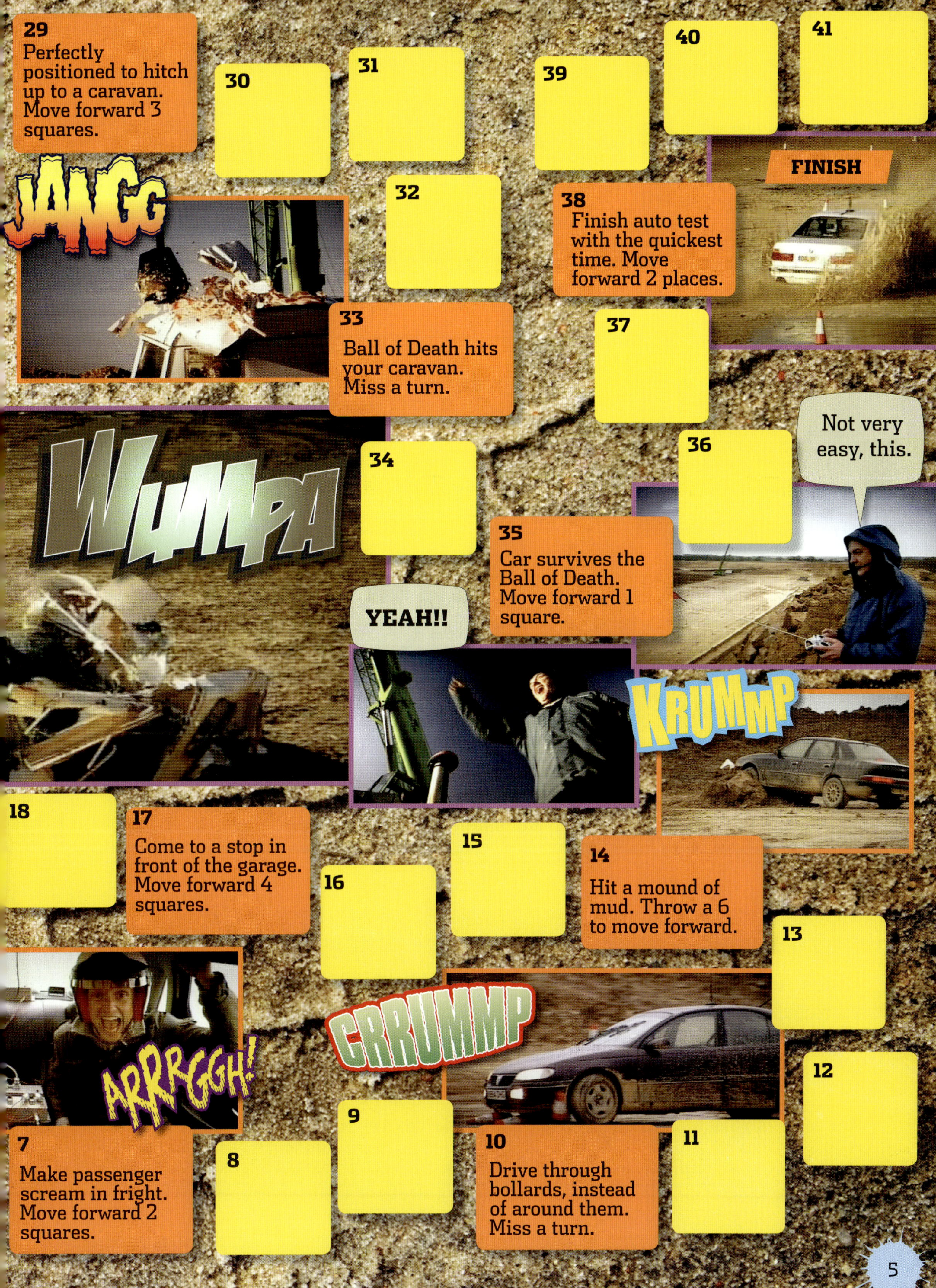

29
Perfectly positioned to hitch up to a caravan. Move forward 3 squares.

30

31

39

40

41

FINISH

32

38
Finish auto test with the quickest time. Move forward 2 places.

33
Ball of Death hits your caravan. Miss a turn.

37

34

35
Car survives the Ball of Death. Move forward 1 square.

36

18

17
Come to a stop in front of the garage. Move forward 4 squares.

16

15

14
Hit a mound of mud. Throw a 6 to move forward.

13

12

7
Make passenger scream in fright. Move forward 2 squares.

8

9

10
Drive through bollards, instead of around them. Miss a turn.

11

Rubbish STUNTS Crossword

Good at cross words, eh? Well, let's see how you get on with this cryptic mish mash.

Clues Across

2. Country where Jeremy raced the Bullet Train. (5)

4. Jeremy tried to turn one of these into a police car. (4,5)

7. This car formed the basis of the Top Gear space shuttle. (7,5)

9. Breed of dog that beat Richard and his Mazda MX5 in a race. (9)

10. Two-wheeler that raced James across Budapest. (3,4)

Clues Down

1. The lads 'enjoyed' taking one of these on holiday to Dorset. (7)

3. Mountains in Europe. (4)

5. The Top Gear team came across a huge one of these in Botswana. (6)

6. They took pot shots at Jeremy as he raced around in a Porsche. (7)

8. The name of the river that a 'tall man' waded across, in a race against James in his Alfa Romeo. (6)

Spot the May

Despite being the only gent on the show who likes to do things properly, James often ends up failing at many of the stunts he attempts. Or losing. Or getting lost.

This time he's definitely the winner. In this page full of Mays can you find the one picture that isn't one of a pair?

Ambitious, but Rubbish

Most cars come in a sporty, fun version where the roof comes off. Most cars apart from MPVs, that is. Until the chaps took a bog-standard Renault Espace and gave it a bit of a makeover... Just how hard could it be to make a convertible MPV?

It was a challenge that involved angle grinders, a sewing machine and a few monkeys. But can you put these shots of the stunt in the correct order?

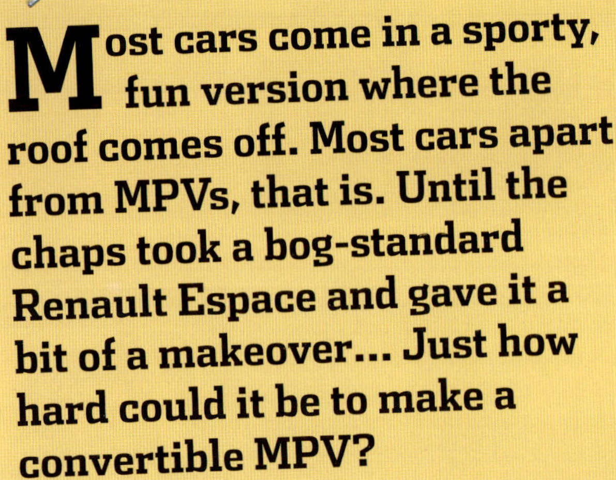

Don't miss out: here's some press-outs so you can create your very own rubbish stunts.
There are boxes to smash through, a ramp to launch off, tyre walls and rally fans to zoom past, and even a caravan and two target cars to aim for. Let the mayhem begin!
*You might need glue and tape for this bit.
RECYCLED PAPER

Get out, get out, get out!
Please can we go?
It looks like someone's Espace has sunk!
KZKZKZKKTZZZ
From a distance, it looks... quite... good...
Behind the wheel of a car like this you feel like you're drowning in wallpaper paste.
You never forget, it's like riding a bicycle.
That's cool – it looks excellent.
g
h
i
j
k
l
m
n

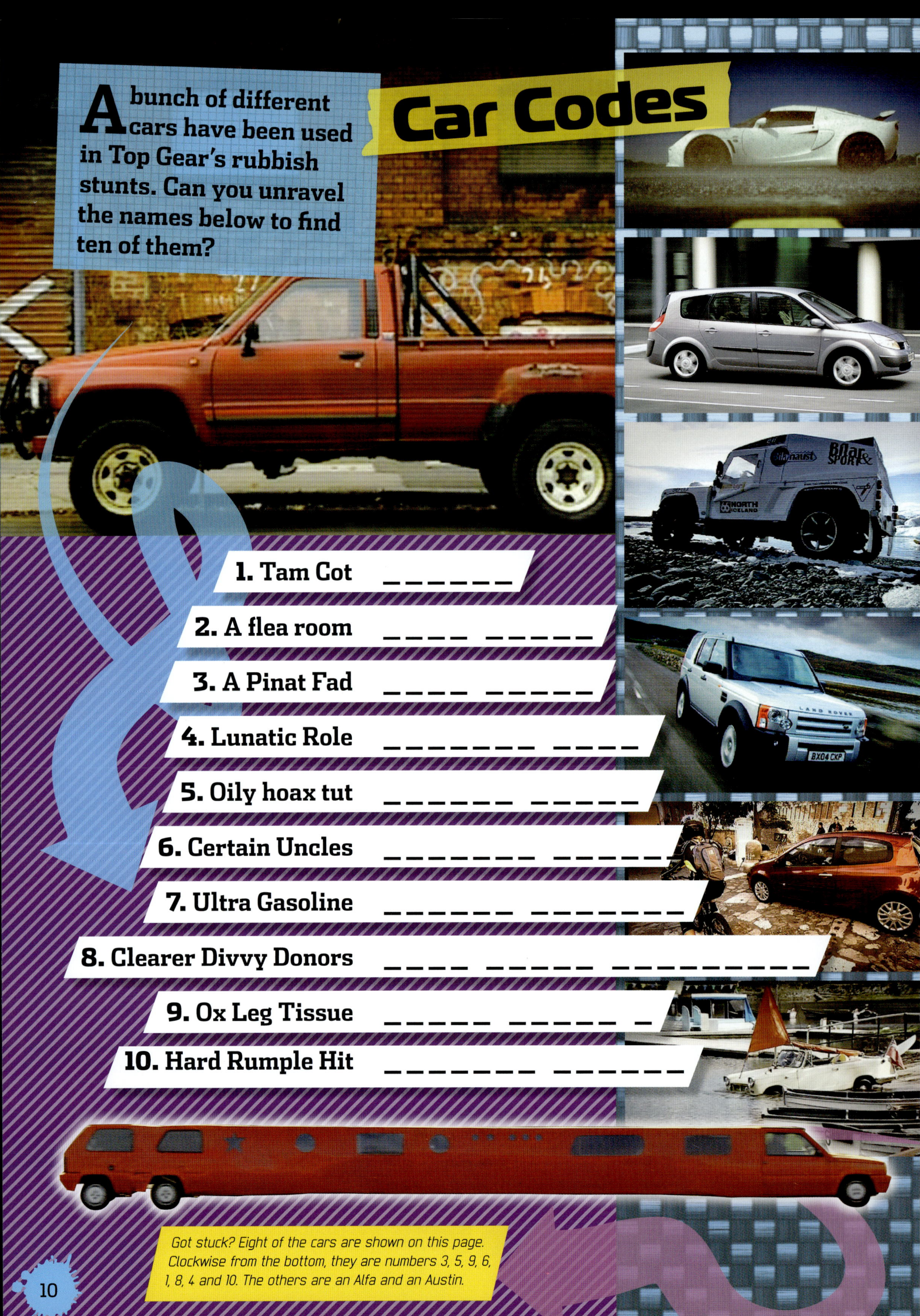

Car Codes

A bunch of different cars have been used in Top Gear's rubbish stunts. Can you unravel the names below to find ten of them?

1. Tam Cot _ _ _ _ _ _

2. A flea room _ _ _ _ _ _ _ _ _

3. A Pinat Fad _ _ _ _ _ _ _ _ _

4. Lunatic Role _ _ _ _ _ _ _ _ _ _ _

5. Oily hoax tut _ _ _ _ _ _ _ _ _ _ _

6. Certain Uncles _ _ _ _ _ _ _ _ _ _ _

7. Ultra Gasoline _ _ _ _ _ _ _ _ _ _ _ _ _

8. Clearer Divvy Donors _ _ _ _ _ _ _ _ _ _ _ _ _ _ _ _ _ _ _

9. Ox Leg Tissue _ _ _ _ _ _ _ _ _ _ _

10. Hard Rumple Hit _ _ _ _ _ _ _ _ _ _ _ _ _

Design A Police Car

Do you remember when the guys had a go at designing police cars? As usual, things didn't go particularly well. Although Jeremy's jazzed-up Fiat Coupe did look the part.

Here is the Lexus James used in the challenge. Can you make it look more police car-ish? Then have a go at drawing your own police car from scratch in the space below...And don't forget to come up with a catchy slogan.

So what exactly happens when a car gets caught in the crosswinds of a Boeing 747? Absolute carnage, as Richard discovered in this mad Top Gear stunt.

There are 7 words hidden in this word search that relate to this stunt, but to make things difficult there are a few extra words thrown in that have absolutely nothing to do with anything. Make sure you find the right ones!

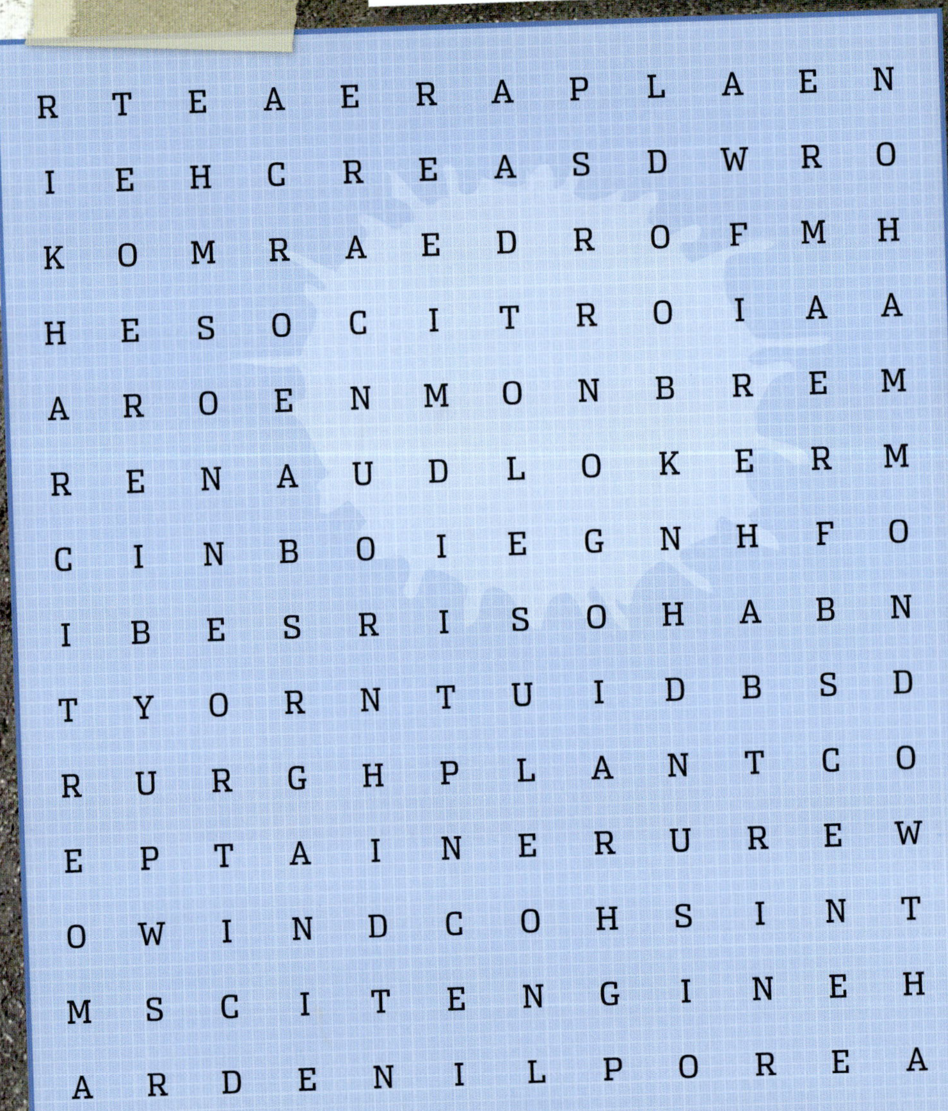

```
R T E A E R A P L A E N
I E H C R E A S D W R O
K O M R A E D R O F M H
H E S O C I T R O I A A
A R O E N M O N B R E M
R E N A U D L O K E R M
C I N B O I E G N H F O
I B E S R I S O H A B N
T Y O R N T U I D B S D
R U R G H P L A N T C O
E P T A I N E R U R E W
O W I N D C O H S I N T
M S C I T E N G I N E H
A R D E N I L P O R E A
```

People Carrier Racing Championship, um…Race.

Six drivers, one finish line. Can you remember who won the first ever people carrier race? Only one MPV's path leads to the finish line. Good luck and remember, no body contact!

Renault Espace + Hammond	Nissan Serena	Mitsubishi Space Wagon	Toyota Space Cruiser	Toyota Previa	Renault Espace

Quiz Time

Whether they're having a go at races or ambitious but rubbish stunts, the chaps are always eager to get on with it. So what are you waiting for? Get on with it!

1. Which of these events didn't happen when our intrepid trio went caravanning in Dorset?
a. The police turned up
b. The Top Gear dog was sick
c. The chemical toilet leaked

2. In which two countries do the team say they'd found the ultimate road?
a. Germany and Austria
b. France and Belguim
c. Switzerland and Italy

3. Who was called 'Officer Barbie' in the Police Car Challenge?
a. Richard
b. James
c. Jeremy

9. Who broke down on a ferry across the Italian lakes?
a. The Stig
b. Richard
c. James

10. What line usually sums up the Top Gear team's attempt at making anything?
a. Ambitious but rubbish
b. Brilliant but flawed
c. Fun but futile

4. When Jeremy re-designed the interior of his Mercedes, which of these wasn't included in the new look?
a. A wooden floor
b. A globe
c. A chandelier

5. 'It's light, it's cheap and it tapers to a point like a rocket.' What classic car was Richard talking about?
a. Reliant Robin
b. Alfa Romeo 159
c. Koenigsegg CCXR

6. What did James flatten while trying to park the caravan in the Caravan Challenge?
a. A washing line
b. A flower bed
c. The tent next door

7. Richard won an extra point for driving through what during the Police Car Challenge?
a. A puddle
b. Some boxes
c. A field of cows

8. What was the nickname given to Jeremy's re-designed Mercedes?
a. Donald Trump Tower
b. Anne Hathaway's Cottage
c. St Paul's Cathedral

See page 16 for the answers

How did you score?

0-3 Hmm, you're a little bit rubbish aren't you? You should probably watch Top Gear every now and then. It's a good show. Honest.

4-6 Better. But your brain still seems on the slow side.

7-9 Very Good. A fine performance, but have another go and see if you can improve.

10 Perfect! You'll be hosting the show in no time!

Answers

Page 2
1. James, 2. Richard, 3. Jeremy, 4. Richard, 5. Jeremy, 6. James, 7. Richard.

Page 3

Page 6
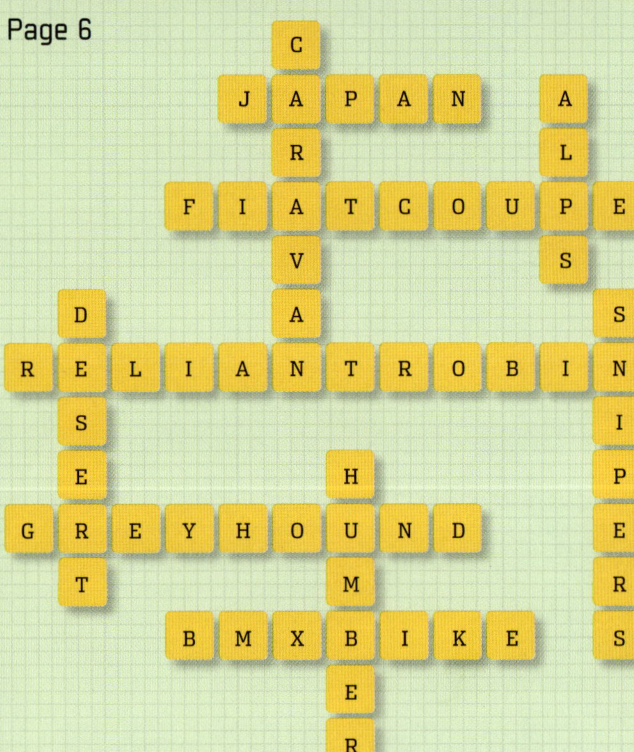

Page 7
There's only one of this particular James May.

Pages 8-9
The correct picture order for the challenge is l-i-j-m-e-n-c-a-b-f-k-g-h-d.

Page 10
1. Tomcat, 2. Alfa Romeo, 3. Fiat Panda, 4. Renault Clio, 5. Toyota Hilux, 6. Renault Scenic, 7. Austin Allegro, 8. Land Rover Discovery, 9. Lotus Exige S, 10, Triumph Herald.

Page 12
The seven words are: Citroen, Boeing, Mondeo, Engine, Ford, Wind, Hammond.

R	T	E	A	E	R	A	P	L	A	E	N
I	E	H	C	R	E	A	S	D	W	R	O
K	O	M	R	A	E	D	R	O	F	M	H
H	E	S	O	C	I	T	R	O	I	A	A
A	R	O	E	N	M	O	N	B	R	E	M
R	E	N	A	U	D	L	O	K	E	R	M
C	I	N	B	O	I	E	G	N	H	F	O
I	B	E	S	R	I	S	O	H	A	B	N
T	Y	O	R	N	T	U	I	D	B	S	D
R	U	R	G	H	P	L	A	N	T	C	O
E	P	T	A	I	N	E	R	U	R	E	W
O	W	I	N	D	C	O	H	S	I	N	T
M	S	C	I	T	E	N	G	I	N	E	H
A	R	D	E	N	I	L	P	O	R	E	A

Page 13

Pages 14-15
1.c, 2.c, 3.a, 4.c, 5.a, 6.c, 7.b, 8.b, 9.c, 10.a.